Verses That Paint A Thousand Tales

Vartika Yadav

Email: authorvartika2024@gmail.com

First Edition , Aug 2024

This book is dedicated to my mother (Mrs.Lalita Yadav) and my aunt (Mausi) (Mrs.Monika Yadav) who have always supported and encouraged me to write this book.

INDEX

GENERAL POEMS

1. The time of childhood 12
2. Sports 14
3. Spirit of Christmas 16
4. Whispers of Spring 18
5. My pet rabbit 20
6. Garden of peace 22
7. Guiding stars in a classroom sky 25
8. Joy of travel 28
9. Nature's Gift 31
10. Life's Melody 33
11. The guiding star 38
12. Friendship 41
13. A teacher's heart 44

FAMILY POEMS

1. My wonderful parents 48
2. My glorious mother 51
3. Dad's Day tribute 53
4. Remembering Goplu: a love beyond borders 56
5. Forever bond by love 60
6. Threads of love and light 63
7. Beacon of love: my great-grandmother (mataji's) grace 66
8. Unbreakable bond 70
9. To my greatest aunt Monika Yadav 73
10. A cousin's eternal bond 76
11. Thank you to my readers 80

General Poems

CHILDHOOD

(MY FIRST POEM WRITTEN IN 2022)

The time of childhood,
the best time indeed.

this time is full of life,
the time to go and thrive.

Going out in the sun,
to have lots of fun.

Rolling in the mud,
Then trolling your mum.

Creeping in the corner ,
And gobbling lots of cookies .

The time of childhood,
the best time indeed.

this time is full of life,
the time to go and thrive.

SPORTS

Sports is just a game ,
It is nothing about fame.

You may win or lose,
It is based on the way you choose.

There is no need to get sad,
There is no need to get mad.

Sports is made for fun,
to play out in the sun.

so let's come out of your
comfort zone,
and play a sport,
to make happiness a fort.

SPIRIT OF CHRISTMAS

In winter's snow and cold so deep,

Comes a time when hearts leap.

It's Christmas time, a special day,
With love and laughter all the way.

Trees adorned with lights that shine,
Stars twinkle, making everything fine.
Gifts wrapped up in ribbons bright,
Bringing smiles of pure delight..

Families gather, hearts unite,
Sharing warmth on this special night.
Eating treats and singing songs,
Celebrating where we belong.

But beyond the gifts and festive
cheer,
Christmas means love, spreading
near.

For kindness and joy, we hold so dear,
Merry Christmas to all, each year!

WHISPERS OF SPRING

The first day of spring, so fresh
and bright,
With flowers waking to the light.

Birds sing sweet songs up in the trees,
And leaves dance gently in the
breeze.

.

The sun shines warmly on the ground,
And life starts growing all around.

Butterflies flutter through the air,
While children play without a care.

Winter's chill is left behind,
New joys and wonders we now find.

The world feels new, so full of cheer,
Spring is here, spring is here!

MY PET RABBIT

In a cozy hutch, fluffy and bright,
my pet rabbit hops with pure delight.

with ear so long and eyes so round,
In my heart he is truly ground.

His fur so soft, a snowy white,
brings me joy from morning to night.
he nibbles on carrots, Munches on hay,
Bringing laughter to each passing day.

With every hop, he spread sheer glee,
His playful antics make me see.
the beauty in simple , Furry Friends,
a bond that never ends.

So here's to my bunny, so dear and sweet,
forever in my heart,
his love will beat.

GARDEN OF PEACE

In a garden full of flowers bright,
lives a butterfly, in the morning light.

It flutters here, it flutters there,
Dancing gently in the air.

The sun is warm the sky is blue,
The grass is green, with drops of dew.
The birds sing songs up in the trees,
Their melodies float on the breeze.

A little stream goes tickling by,
With shiny pebbles, low and high.
The fish swims in its clear cool flow,
Their scales like silver in the glow.

Children laugh and run around,
Their feet make soft thumps on the
ground.

They pickup stones and throw them far,
They spread joy,each passing hour.

The flowers sway,they gently greet,
Each buzzing bee , they chase to meet.
They open wide to face the day,
And smile as sunshine lights their way.

At night the stars shine up above,
The moonlight baths the world in
love.
The garden rests so still and calm,
Wrapped in nature's gentle balm.

GUIDING STARS IN A CLASSROOMS SKY

In a classroom bathed in morning light,
Two guiding stars, so brilliant and bright,
2 wonderful teachers, dear,
Taught me wonders, year after year.

A teacher, with wisdom's gentle grace,
Unfurled the world in a warm embrace,
Her voice a melody of soft delight,
Guiding each step, day and night.

In every lesson, a spark she'd sow,
With patience endless, her passion would show,
From numbers and letters to dreams unseen,
She painted knowledge in colors serene.

And the other, with a spark so keen,
Unveiled the magic in the mundane scene,
Her teachings were songs of joy and cheer,

Turning each challenge into something
clear.

With hands that sculpted skills anew,
She helped us see the world in hues,
Of creativity, logic, and boundless flair,
A mentor's touch beyond compare.

Together, they crafted a canvas bright,
Where knowledge and wisdom took flight,
With every lesson, every gentle nudge,
They taught me to dream, to strive, to
judge.

In the tapestry of life, their threads
entwine,
In every success, their teachings shine.
the two teachers are, forever
dear,
In every heart, their wisdom will appear.

JOY OF TRAVEL

Travel far or travel near,
So many places,so much cheer.

Walk in the streets of your hometown,
Feel the life all around.

Ride the bus or catch a train,
Watch the world through the window pane.
Mountains, rivers, trees so tall,
Nature's wonders, see them all.

Fly across the oceans wide,
New country on the other side.
Different people different ways,
New food to try, new games to play.

Castles, beaches,city lights,
Amazing views and starry nights.
Learn a new word hear a new song,
Make new friends as you go along.

Travel brings a special joy,
For every girl and every boy.
Memories made and stories to share,
Travel shows how much we care.

So pack your bags, don't delay,
Big adventure is on its way.
Near or far, day or night,
Travel filles our hearts with light.

NATURE'S GIFT

Nature's embrace, a symphony of hues,
wherever you gaze, vibrant views.

Dense forest whisper, secrets untold ,
Planes unfold, a tapestry gold .

Greenery blankets the Earth sweet skin,
Nature's nourishment a dance within.

Orange sunset a fiery Delight,
Blue skies, a canvas of infinite height.

Pink blooms, a torch of Grace,
in this Paradise, life find its place

LIFE'S MELODY

In the morning, when the light is bright,
A new day starts ,so fresh and light.

People hurry, off they go,
In the busy streets they flow.
But I take a moment, calm and slow,
To watch the trees and feel the glow.

Life is short, so make it bright,
Love and laughter with all your might.
Each day's a gift so live it well,
In every moment ,let your heart swell.

Things around me ,big and small,
like a book, or my favourite ball.
they tell me stories, keep my dreams,
silent friend, or so it seems.

My old guitar, with strings so thin ,
plays songs of now, and songs of then.
each music strum a memory , a friends
touch,

Music's Magic means so much.

Birds sing songs, the sun comes up,
A happy tune fills my cup.

I get out of my bed,stretch,and yawn,
Ready to see what is going on.
I smell the coffee warm and sweet,
A morning treat that is hard to beat.

The sun climbs higher in the sky,
As time ticks by,hours fly.
Music plays ,my friend all day,
It makes me smile,it leads the way.

Songs of love and dreams come true,
Music helps when I feel blue.

It's rhythm flows,so soft and kind,
A gentle hug for heart and mind.

The clock ticks on , the day moves fast,
moments blend, and memories last.
Simple Joys and laughter shared,
show how much we truly cared.

as a sun sets and the night is near,
The stars above seem so clear.
I think of all the day has shown,
the simple truth I have known.

forgive the hurts, let go of pain,
to hold a grudge is not to gain.
Forgiving frees you, makes you strong,
helps you move and dance along.

life is a journey quick and Grand,
with highs and lows, we understand.

so live it fully , come what may,
and embrace each moment of the day

in laughter's Echo, in sorrows sigh,
and every tear and every high.
life is short, but rich and sweet,
a wondrous Journey, a special treat.

Laugh and dance, sing and play,
find the beauty in everyday.
for life is short, but oh so sweet,
a wondrous journey, a special treat.

so here's to days both calm and wild,
the moments Grand and simply mild.
to live fully come what may,
embracing all within each day.

THE GUIDING STAR

In classrooms bright where dreams take flight,

You light the way, you shine so bright.

With every word and every smile,
You make each day so worthwhile.

Through endless days and tireless nights,
You guide us to reach new heights.
With lessons crafted from the heart,
You give each student a brand-new start.

You see the good in every soul,
And help us strive to reach our goal.
With gentle hands and open mind,
You teach us all to be so kind.

Your wisdom flows, your patience endless,
Your spirit strong, your heart so boundless.
In every subject, every theme,
You help us all to dare to dream.

For every challenge faced with grace,
You make the world a better place.

With every laugh and every cheer,
You make our path ahead so clear.

So here's to you, our guiding star,
Who's led us from both near and far.
We thank you for your endless care,
For always being there.

May your days be filled with peace and light,
And may your heart always feel right.
For you have touched so many lives,
And in your glow, our spirit thrives.

Written with love for my brilliant class teacher Mrs. Praveen

FRIENDSHIP

In the world of friends, we stand tall
Through thick and thin, we never fall.

A friend is like a shining light,
Guiding us through the darkest night

.

They laugh with us, wipe our tears away,
In their company, we always find our way
They listen to our stories, big and small,
And lift us up whenever we fall.

With friends, we share our joy and sorrow,
Knowing they'll be there, today and tomorrow.
They make us smile when we feel blue,
Their friendship is forever true.

In times of trouble, they lend a hand,
Together, we bravely make a stand.
For in the bond of friendship, we find,
Strength and love that's one of a kind.

So here's to friends, both near and far,
You're the brightest, shiniest star.
In this journey of life, till the very end,
With friends like you, we'll always
transcend.

A TEACHER'S HEART

In a world of books and lessons planned,
With chalk and markers in your hand,

You shape the minds of future's grace,
And guide them to a brighter place.

With patience vast and wisdom deep,
You plant the dreams that children keep.
Through every challenge, every test,
You bring out each student's best.

A beacon in the darkest night,
You fill our minds with wondrous light.
You see the spark in every child,
And fan the flames until they're wild.

In every story, every fact,
You weave a tale that stays intact.
With every lesson, every day,
You help the lost to find their way.

For all the times you've stayed up late,
To plan and grade and contemplate,

For every tear and every smile,
You make each moment so worthwhile.

So here's to you, dear teacher friend,
Whose dedication knows no end.
We thank you for the love you share,
For always being kind and fair.

May your days be filled with joy and peace,
And may your passion never cease.
For in your care, we find our start,
You are the teacher with a kind heart.

Written with love for amazing class teacher Miss. Shivani

Family Poems

MY WONDERFUL PARENTS

In the world of love, my parents stand tall,

Guiding me, caring for me through it all.

They laugh with me, they cry with me too,
Their love's strong, always shining through.

With hugs and cuddles, they make me feel safe,
Their love's like a warm, cozy place.
Through tough times and days that are bright,
They're by my side, holding me tight.

Their love teaches me to be kind and true,
To chase my dreams, whatever I pursue
With patience and love, they help me learn,
To face each challenge, to take each turn.

Their smiles light up my every day,
Chasing the shadows, keeping fears at bay.

In their eyes, I see hopes and dreams,
Their love's a river, flowing in endless streams.

So here's to my wonderful mom and dad,
Whose love makes me happy, never sad.
In their arms, I find my home sweet,
Forever grateful, in their love I meet .

Written with love for the best parents in the world

MY GLORIOUS MOTHER

In a world so big, so wide, so Grand,
stands my mother, with a gentle hand.

her love a light that always shines,
guiding me through life designs.

with arms so warm, heart's so true,
She is always there, whatever I do.
her smile a beacon at night,
fills my world with pure delight.

she works so hard, without complaints,
her strength, of course never faints.
in her embrace, I find my peace,
her love for me will never cease.

My glorious mother, oh so dear,
with you, I have nothing to fear.
thank you for all that you do,
my love for you is forever true.

Written with love for my wonderful mother

DAD'S DAY TRIBUTE

In your arms, I always found,
A place where love knows no bound..

With your smile, my fears would fade,
In your strength, I felt unafraid.

You taught me to dream, to aim high,
To reach for the stars in the sky.
With your wisdom, I found my way,
In your words, I learned to stay.

Through your eyes, I saw the light,
In your heart, everything felt right.
Your hands held me steady and true,
In your love, I always grew.

For all the times you made me smile,
For the moments that went the extra mile,
I thank you, Dad, with all my heart,
For being there from the very start.

On this special day, I want to say,
I love you more than words can say.

Happy Father's Day to the best dad,
In your love, I feel truly blessed.

Written with love for my superhero father

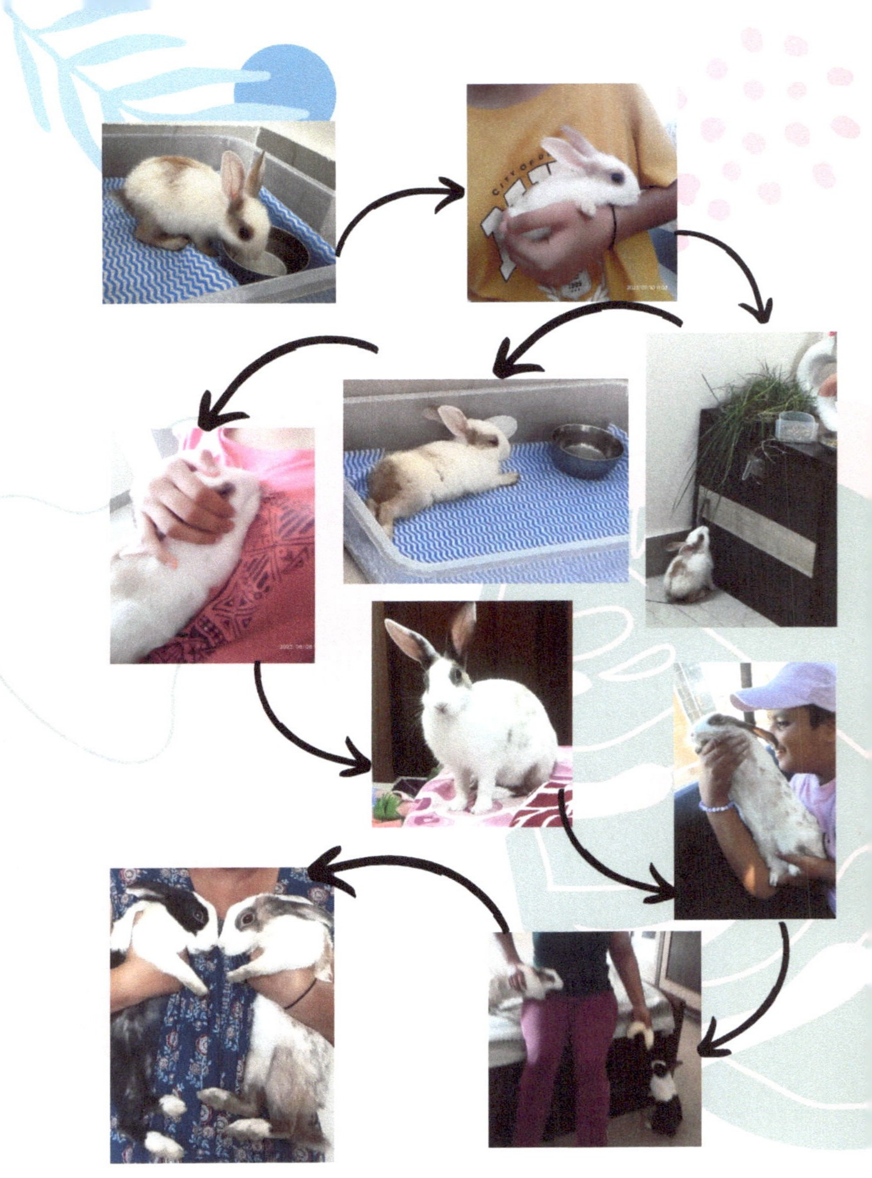

REMEMBERING GOPLU:A LOVE BEYOND BORDERS

In the quiet of our humble home, a tale of love unfolds,
A rabbit named Goplu, with a heart of gold,
For my sister's yearning, not a dog or cat,
But a little fluffy bunny, we tenderly pat.

White and beige, a sight to behold,
At merely 25 days, our hearts he stole,
Only we three, my mother, sister, and I,
Could understand Goplu's secret sigh.

To the park, we'd journey, hand in paw,
Watching him prance with gentle awe,
He'd nibble on grass, savoring the taste,
And vegetables fresh, never in haste.

With a gentle touch, we'd massage his head,

A signal of love, till the day he was fed,
In his gaze, we saw a world unspoken,
A bond of joy, never to be broken.

Yet life led us, to lands afar,
Leaving Goplu behind, a tender scar,
Our tears did flow, a river of sorrow,
As we left him for a distant morrow.

To keep him whole, another we got,
A friend for Goplu, our hearts were fought,
At a farmhouse safe, they now reside,
While oceans apart, our hearts confide.

In video calls, we see him still,
Our love for Goplu, no distance can kill,
For in our hearts, he is crowned and dear,
A memory eternal, always near.

Oh Goplu, though far away you roam,
In our hearts, you are safely home,
No matter where this journey leads,
Your love plants deeply rooted seeds.

Written with love for my cutest bunny

FOREVER BOND BY LOVE

In days of youth, when I was small,
And she was five, so brave and tall,

She helped our mother every day,
And Dad abroad, far away.

She played with me, a guiding light,
In shadows cast by the darkest night,
Memories shared, both laugh and cry,
Together we would reach the sky.

A pillar strong, my sister dear,
She stands with me, always near.
Through storms and trials, brave and true,
She fought for me, our bond anew.

Her strength, her courage, shining bright,
She comforts me with all her might,
Now at eleven, hand in hand,
Our bond's unbreakable, we stand.

Through joy and sorrow, side by side,
In her embrace, I do confide,

For she, my sister, heart so pure,
Our love, forever will endure.

Written with love for my charming sister(Angel)

THREADS OF LOVE AND LIGHT

In the warmth of home, where love resides,

My heart finds peace, my soul abides.
A mother's touch, so soft, so kind,
In her embrace, true love I find.

Her gentle words, her soothing care,
A comfort that's beyond compare.
Through every storm, she's by my side,
A guiding light, a constant guide.

A father's strength, so firm and true,
His wisdom leads me in all I do.
With hands that build and arms that hold,
In his care, I grow strong and bold.

He's taught me courage, grace, and more,
A beacon in life's endless shore.
With every step, I feel his pride,
A bond so deep, none can divide.

An elder sister, wise and dear,
Her laughter chases every fear.

She's walked the path I now explore,
Her lessons make me strong, and secure.

She shares with me her dreams, her ways,
And brightens all my darkest days.
In her, I find a friend so true,
A sister's love, forever new.

Together, we are bound by love,
A gift from heaven up above.
In their care, I find my way,
A family's love, come what may.

Written with love for the best family

"BEACON OF LOVE: MY GREAT-GRANDMOTHER'S (MATAJI'S) GRACE"

In childhood's tender, fleeting days,
A beacon shone through mist and haze.
My great-grandmother, heart so kind,
A gentle guide where strength combined.

When mother worked and father was
away,
Sister but five, a world unknown.
She taught me first to walk, then run,
And shared sweet tales 'til day was done.

Her stories wove life's lessons deep,
In parks where memories softly sleep.
Among the trees, the laughter rang,
With every step, my heart she sang.

Though family ties seemed frail and thin,
Her love was light that shone within.
Her calls of care, without disdain,
No words of chide, no hint of strain.

At eleven now, I clearly see,
Her love unwavering, wild and free.
A joy she finds in our delight,
Her presence is warm, our guiding
light.

When my great-grandmother is near,
There's no need for me to fear.
Grandma (Mataji), is always so
supportive and kind,
With her, comfort and strength I find.

In the park, when alone I'd stay,
She'd tell others, "Let her play."
(अरे म्हारी जीजी ने भी खिलाओ)
In every quarrel, by my side, she stood,
Her words made me feel understood.

"You're a brave girl," she'd always say,
"Don't fear anyone, come what may.

For with you, I'll always be,
To guard and guide, eternally."

Her love, a shield, her spirit bright,
Making everything seem right.
With great grandma (Mataji) all my fears disappear,
In her presence, I'm brave and clear.

The greatest great-grandmother's grace,
A lasting smile upon her face.
A helping hand, a beacon true,
Grandma, my heart belongs to you.

Written with love for my great-grand mother(Mataji) who has always supported our family ,and especially my mother.

UNBREAKABLE BOND

Sejal, my dear cousin, so bright,
We talk and share, day and night.

In joy and sorrow, side by side,
Together, we take every stride.

Laughter echoes, memories sweet,
In every moment, our hearts meet.
Through highs and lows, we hold tight,
Guiding each other with love's light.

When tears fall, and smiles fade,
We find comfort in the shade.
Hand in hand, we face the rain,
In each other, we find no pain.

Happy times and days so warm,
Together, we weather every storm.
Dreams we weave, hopes we share,
Knowing we will always care.

Through thick and thin, we stand tall,
For each other, we give our all.

In Sejal, I found a friend,
A bond that will never end.

Thank you, Sejal, for being you,
For making our world bright and true.
In joy and sorrow, always through,
My love for you forever grew.

Written with love for my best cousin (Sejal)

TO MY GREATEST AUNT MONIKA

In the days when I was just a baby,

You cradled me with love so steady.
To movies, games, and tasty treats,
Creating memories is oh-so-sweet.

Laughter echoed through the days,
As you both found endless ways,
To fill the hours with endless fun,
Beneath the warm and shining sun.

And as I grew, I joined the ride,
With you and Sis right by my side,
We shared in moments, big and small,
And built a bond that would not fall.

Now older, wiser, still we stand,
Guided by your loving hand,
You offer wisdom, pure and true,
And show us what we ought to do.

For the book I've written, thanks to you,
And Mom, who's always seen me through,

You've been my beacon, shining bright,
Guiding me towards the light.
So here's my thanks, deep and sincere,
For all you've done, for being near,
In every chapter, in every line,
Your love and support eternally shine.

Written with love for my Incredible aunt Monika

A COUSIN'S ETERNAL BOND

In a world so bright with laughter and cheer,

A little cousin named Ayaan, so dear.
At four years old, his heart so pure,
In the embrace of family, his joy is sure.

With me and my sister, he'd always play,
Sharing joys and fun, day after day.
His eyes sparkled more for my sister,
it's true, In every little fight, her side,
he'd choose.

On her bed, he'd let her rest,
While I'd have to move, at his gentle
request.
But as her time was taken by studies
and books,
Ayaan's eyes sought another familiar
nook.

He turned to me, with a smile so wide,
Together we played, side by side.

Equally now his love would flow,
For both of us, his heart would glow.

Though friends, excluded him, he tried his best,
Sharing toys, enduring every test.
But those children were mean, they'd push him away,
Yet in our hearts, he would always stay.

Time passed, we had to part,
To a land abroad, breaking his young heart.
But distance couldn't dim the bond so true,
In hearts and calls, our love only grew.

He saved candies and chocolates, sweets and fair,

Gifts and cards, showing how much
he cared.
His love, a treasure, a binding thread,
Connecting us, where our paths had led.

Now with new friends, his laughter bright,
Ayaan is happy, under the sunlight.
Joyful and free, his spirit soars,
With love that echoes forevermore.

No matter where we are, near or far,
Our hearts remain, a guiding star.
For sweet Ayaan, our love will never fade,
In memories cherished, and bonds so
well-made.

Written with love for my most adorable and cutest cousin (Ayaan)

A THANK YOU TO MY READERS

To you, my readers, I want to say,

Thank you for joining me each day.

Your support means the world to me,
In every word and line you see.

You turn the pages, read each part
With open mind and open heart.
Your kindness shines through every view,
Making what I write feel new.

In every story, rhyme, or prose,
Your encouragement truly shows.
It gives me strength to carry on,
To write each night and every dawn.

So here's a heartfelt thanks to you,
For seeing my stories through and through.
Your loyalty and love inspire,
Setting my writer's heart on fire.

Thank you, readers, near and far,
For being just the way you are.
Your support is my guiding light,
Making each word I write feel right.

SPECIAL THANKS...

I want to express my heartfelt gratitude to the two incredible teachers at Alpine Convent School who have played pivotal roles in my journey as a writer.

To Ms.Shivani who illuminated the path to my hidden talent, your insight and guidance have opened doors I never knew existed.

To Mrs.Praveen, who has been a constant source of encouragement, thank you for always believing in my words and pushing me to share them with the world. Your unwavering support in my poetry has inspired me to take this leap and publish my work. Without your motivation, this book would not have come to life.

www.ingramcontent.com/pod-product-compliance
Lightning Source LLC
LaVergne TN
LVHW021257160826
845679LV00001B/118

* 9 7 9 8 8 9 5 5 6 4 4 4 8 *